SCHIRMER'S LIBRARY
OF MUSICAL CLASSICS

HENRY SCHRADIECK

The School of Violin-Technics

→ BOOK I

Exercises for Promoting Dexterity in the Various Positions

Library Vol. 515

BOOK II

Exercises in Double-Stops

Library Vol. 516

BOOK III

Exercises in the Different Modes of Bowing

Library Vol. 517

G. SCHIRMER, Inc.

DISTRIBUTED BY

HAL•LEONARD®
CORPORATION

7777 W. BLUEMOUND RD. P.O. BOX 13819 MILWAUKEE, WI 53213

Printed In the U. S. A.

The School of Violin-Technics.

Section I.

Exercises for promoting Dexterity in the various Positions.

I.

Exercises on One String.

The pupil should be careful in all the exercises to keep the hand perfectly quiet, letting the fingers fall strongly, and raising them with elasticity.

The tempo must be lessened or accelerated, according to the ability of the pupil, but is generally moderate.

II.

III.
Exercises on Two Strings.

IV.

Exercises to be practised with wrist-movement only, keeping the right arm perfectly quiet.

V.
Exercises on Three Strings.

VI.
Exercises on Four Strings.

VII.

VIII.
Exercises in the Second Position.

IX.

Exercises in the First and Second Positions.

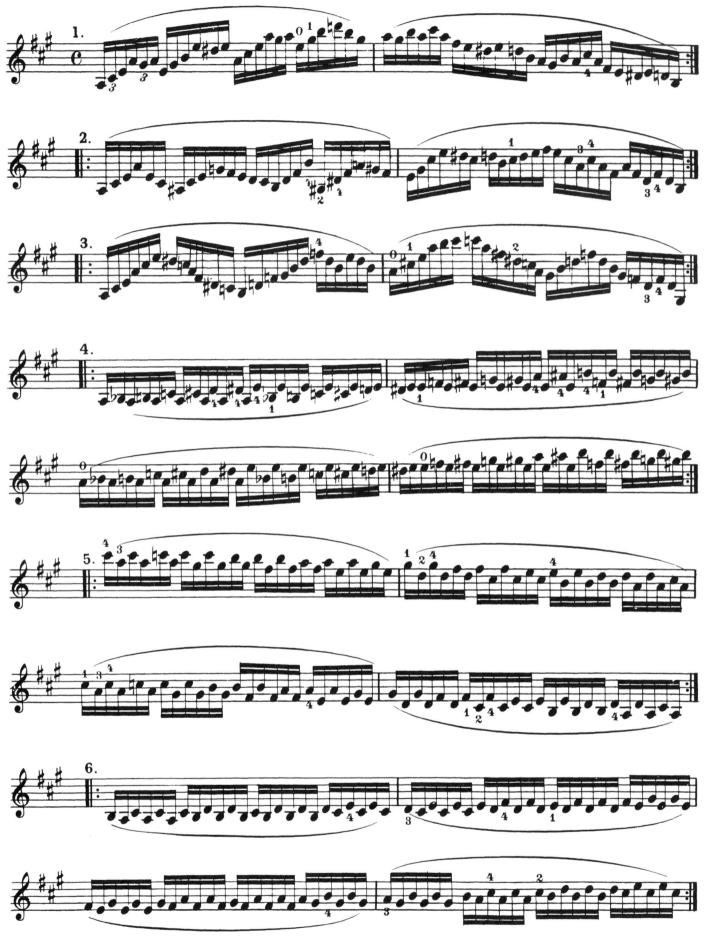

X.
Exercises in the Third Position.

XI.

Exercises in the First, Second and Third Positions.

XII.
Exercises in the Fourth Position.

XIII.

Exercises on the First, Second, Third and Fourth Positions.

XIV.

Exercises in the Fifth Position.

XV.

Exercises passing through Five Positions.

XVI.
Exercises in the Sixth Position.

XVII.

Exercises passing through Six Positions.

XVIII.

Exercises in the Seventh Position.

XIX.

XX.

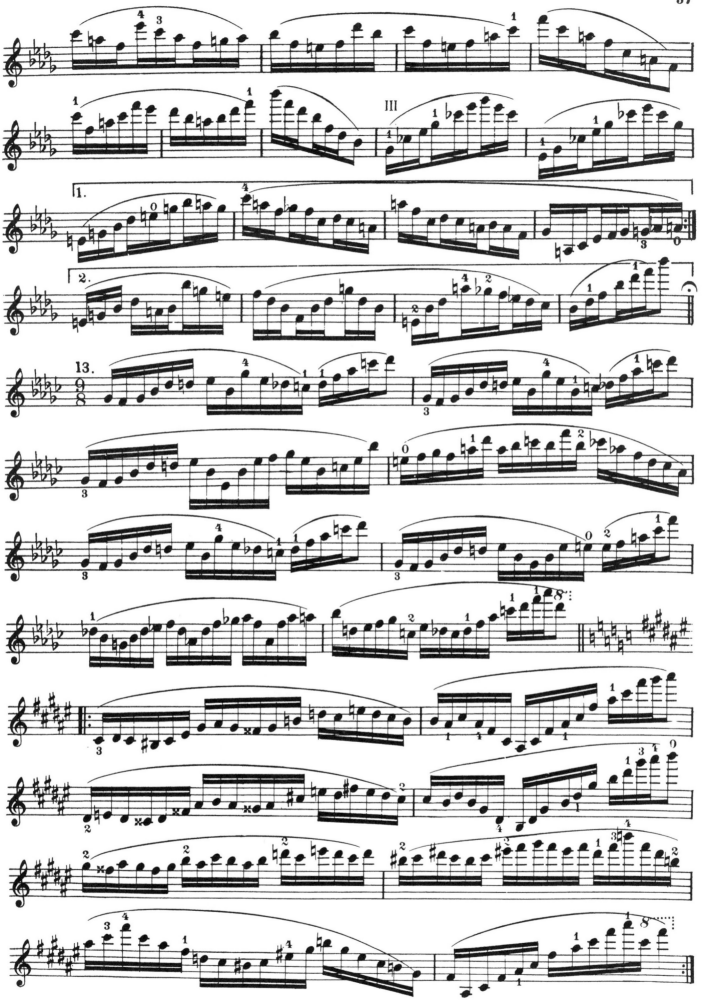

38

14. Allegro vivace.

15. Energico.

43